EDVARD GRIEG

SOLVEJGS LIED

für Gesang und Klavier
for Voice and Piano

Original-Ausgabe / Original Edition

EIGENTUM DES VERLEGERS · ALLE RECHTE VORBEHALTEN
ALL RIGHTS RESERVED

C. F. PETERS

FRANKFURT/M. · LEIPZIG · LONDON · NEW YORK

Aufführungsmaterial zur Orchesterfassung (vom Komponisten) lieferbar.
Material for performance of the orchestral version
(completed by the composer) available.

SOLVEJGS LIED

Henrik Ibsen

Edvard Grieg (1843–1907)
Deutsche Übersetzung von W. Henzen
English translation by E. M. Smyth
Französisch von Frank van der Stucken

Un poco Andante

Der Win-ter mag schei-den, der Früh-ling ver-geh'n, der Früh-ling ver-geh'n, der
The win-ter may pass and the spring dis-ap-pear, the spring dis-ap-pear, the
L'hi-ver peut s'en-fuir, le prin-temps bien-ai-mé Peut s'é-cou-ler; Les

Edition Peters Nr. 2453a

7236

Sommer mag verwelken, das Jahr verwehn, das Jahr verwehn; du kehrest mir zurücke, gewiss, du wirst mein, gewiss, du wirst mein, ich hab' es versprochen, ich harre treulich dein, ich harre treulich dein. *(vor sich hin summend:)* A—

summer too will vanish and then the year, and then the year. But this I know for certain: thou'lt come back again, thou'lt come back again; and e'en as I promised, thou'lt find me waiting then, thou'lt find me waiting then. (humming:) Ah!

feuilles d'automne et les fruits de l'été, Tout peut passer. Mais tu me reviendras, o mon doux fiancé, Pour ne plus me quitter: Je t'ai donné mon coeur, il attend résigné Et ne pourrait changer. (fredonnant:) A—

Allegretto con moto

pp una corda

Tempo I

Gott hel-fe dir, wenn du die Son-ne noch siehst, die Son-ne noch siehst. Gott
God help thee, when wan-d'ring thy way all a-lone, thy way all a-lone, God
Que Dieu veuille en-cor, dans sa gran-de bon-té, Te pro-té-ger Au pa-

segne dich, wenn du zu Füssen ihm kniet, zu Füssen ihm kniet.
grant to thee His strength, as thou kneel'st at His throne, thou kneel'st at His throne.
ys loin tain qui te tient e-xi-lé Loin du fo-yer.

poco animato

Ich will deiner har-ren, bis du mir nah', bis du mir nah', und har-rest du dort o-ben, so
If thou now art wai-ting in heav'n for me, in heav'n for me, o there we'll meet a-gain love and
Moi, je t'at-tends i-ci, cher et doux fi-an-cé, Jus-qu'à mon jour der-nier; Je t'ai don-né mon coeur plein

poco sostenuto

tref-fen wir uns da, so tref-fen wir uns da! A—
never par-ted be, and never par-ted be! Ah!
de fi-dé-li-té: Il ne pour-rait chan-ger. A—

Allegretto con moto
pp una corda
Ped.
3
Tempo I
pp
pp
tre corde
p
dim.
pp